CAN THE POLICE LIE TO ME?

150 Things You Need To Know about Police, Prosecutors and Criminal Law

Copyright Ralph S. Behr, Esq.
888 S.E. Third Ave., Suite 400
Fort Lauderdale, Florida 33316
Telephone: 954-761-3444   1-800-761-3446
To Contact the Author go to:
www//ralphbehr.com

Library of Congress cataloging –in-Publication Data:
ISBN-13: 978-1-60402-942-0

14,094,186 Americans arrested last year!*

30,000,000 had "police contact"!

50,000,000 traffic citations!

Every one of us has constitutional rights.

The right to be protected from unreasonable searches and seizures, the right to confront our accusers, the right to a jury trial, the right to due process, equal protection of the law, the right to an attorney.

Few of us fully understand what those rights mean.
How they are enforced by the courts.
How they are often abused by the police and prosecutors.

Now you will know.

You can protect yourself with information and knowledge.

* Source U.S. Government U.S. Department of Justice

Dear Reader:

Thousands of people have gone to prison, although innocent. This was demonstrated by law professor Brandon L. Garrett, whose systematic examination of a sample of 200 cases concluded that innocent persons served an average of 12 years in prison.

Prosecutors exercise vast powers, too often abusively. They have almost unlimited tax money, the police, and a staff of investigators. The defendant has only a limited amount of money, if any at all. Without effective representation, you will be ground-up by the system.

To save himself, an accused person must rely on his lawyer.

If you, or someone close to you, is the subject of a police investigation, or is being prosecuted, hire an experienced criminal defense attorney.

Your freedom and liberty can be gained, or lost, based on the experience and effectiveness of your lawyer.

This book is not a substitute for a lawyer, nor should it be relied upon in making legal decisions. Only a licensed attorney can advise and represent you.

Ralph S. Behr, Esq.
Fort Lauderdale, FL

FOR MORE INFORMATION GO TO: *www//ralphbehr.com*

THIS BOOK HAS TWO PARTS

Part I   CRIMES

50 *'most charged'* crimes defined

Part II ANSWERS

100 *'most asked'* questions answered

50 *'most charged'* crimes defined

50 *most charged* crimes defined

100 '*most asked*' questions

CARS AND COPS

DRUG BUSTS

100 'most asked' questions

FOR THE UNDER 21 CROWD

SEARCHES

100 *'most asked'* questions

can my boss look in my desk?   97
can my boss listen to my phone calls?   98
can a teacher search a student's locker?   99
can the police search me on someone's lie?   100
what is plain view?   101

POLICE CONTACT

do I have to talk to the police?   104
can I try to make a deal with the police?   105
can the police stop me on the street?   106
why is the cop talking to me?   107
can I walk away from a police officer?   108
is it a crime to refuse to give information?   109
can I refuse to give a cop my name?   110
do I have to tell them what I know?   111
am I obstructing justice by not answering?   112
what should I do if I am being questioned?   113
can I talk a cop into not arresting me?   114
is a rent-a-cop a real cop?   115
should I open the door if the police knock?   116
can I ask an undercover cop if he's a cop?   117
what if I run?   118
can the police lie to me?   119

x

100 '*most asked*' questions

ARRESTS

100 *'most asked'* questions

BAIL

WHO DECIDES?

100 *most asked* questions

DISCOVERY

DEFENSES

100 *most asked* questions

TRIAL

SENTENCING

100 *most asked* questions

CRIMES
50 *'most charged'* crimes defined

CHAPTER SYLLABUS:

SIMPLE AND CONCISE DEFINITIONS OF THE 50 MOST

OFTEN CHARGED CRIMINAL OFFENSES FILED BY

PROSECUTORS IN THE UNITED STATES

CRIMES

50 'most charged' crimes defined

WHAT IS A CRIME?

"Crime" means a felony or a misdemeanor.

Violations and infractions are not defined as crimes.

There are no "common law" crimes. That means that you cannot be arrested for bad behavior. You can only be arrested and charged with violating a written criminal law.

Only the legislature can create criminal statutes. Courts and the police cannot create a "new" crime.

You can only be convicted if the state can prove you committed each and every element of the crime.

Failure to allege and prove each and every element will result in an acquittal.

CRIMES
50 'most charged' crimes defined

WHAT IS A MISDEMEANOR?

A misdemeanor is any crime which is punishable by a stay in the county jail of up to 364 days.

You go to jail for violating a misdemeanor statute.

You go to prison for violating a felony statute.

You do not loose your civil rights if you are convicted of a misdemeanor charge. Unless the misdemeanor a crime of dishonesty (such as theft) it does not affect your ability to obtain a license in most professions.

Although you can be placed on probation for misdemeanor, a maximum period of probation can not be greater than one year.

If you violate any conditions of misdemeanor probation the judge can send you to jail for a maximum of one year.

In most states conviction of two misdemeanor theft charges can result in a felony theft charge for any subsequent theft arrest.

CRIMES

50 *'most charged'* crimes defined

WHAT IS A FELONY?

A felony is any crime which is punishable by one year or more in prison.

Felonies are divided into degrees.

Felonies also carry a loss of civil rights:

-the right to vote
-the right to hold elected office
-the right to own a firearm
-some require you register with the local sheriff
-some professions disqualify felons.

In several states conviction of a sex crime or sexually motivated crime can result in civil commitment after incarceration. Civil commitment means you can be returned to prison for indefinite term if a jury finds you a continuing risk of recidivism for sex crimes.

CRIMES

ACCESSORY AFTER THE FACT

To prove this crime the state must prove that *after* the felony was committed you:

1. assisted or gave aid,
2. knowing the other person committed a felony
3. that you intended to help that person avoid detection, or escape,
4. you are not related by blood or marriage.

CRIMES

ARSON

Arson is the damage of property by fire or explosion. For it to be a crime the state has to prove:

1. There was damage to a structure or dwelling, caused by fire or explosion.

2. The damage was done willfully, or during the commission of another felony.

CRIMES
50 'most charged' crimes defined

ASSAULT

An "assault" is an intentional, unlawful threat by word or act to do violence to the person of another, coupled with an apparent ability to do so, and doing some act which creates a well-founded fear that violence is imminent.

The word assault is often confused with the word battery. They have quite different meanings in law.

The thing to keep in mind is that a battery is an unlawful touching. An assault is putting someone in fear of an unlawful touching.

To prove the crime of Assault the state must prove:

1. The defendant intentionally and unlawfully threatened, either by word or act, to do violence to the victim.
2. At the time the defendant appeared to have the ability to carry out the threat.
3. The act of the defendant created in the mind of the victim a well-founded fear that the violence was about to take place.

BATTERY

A battery is an unlawful touching.

The state must prove:

The defendant intentionally touched or struck the victim against his/her will.

A battery may become a felony when the touching causes serious bodily harm.

CRIMES

BOOKMAKING

The elements are:

1. Defendant was engaged in the business or profession of gambling.
2. While so engaged he/she took or received a bet or wager.
3. The bet or wager was upon the result of any trial or contest, or skill, speed, power or endurance of human, beast, fowl, motor vehicle or mechanical apparatus, or upon the result of any change, casualty, unknown, or contingent event.

CRIMES

BRIBERY

To corruptly give, offer, or promise to any public servant any pecuniary or other benefit with the intent to influence the performance of any act within the discretion or power of the public servant.

The state must prove:

1. The defendant directly or indirectly gave or offered something of value to a public official.
2. The defendant did so knowingly and corruptly, with the intent to influence an official act.

CRIMES
50 *'most charged'* crimes defined

BURGLARY

Burglary is trespass PLUS an additional criminal act. The intent to commit a criminal act <u>must</u> have been formed <u>before</u> the trespass for the charge of burglary to be proven.

There are different punishments for different fact patterns. Burglary of an occupied dwelling at night with a weapon can be a life felony.

Burglary of an unoccupied building or car is a lesser felony.

To convict someone of burglary the state must prove:

1. An entering of a structure, vehicle or trespass on land.
2. The entering was without permission of the owner.
3. At the time of the entering the defendant had the fully-formed conscious intent to commit a crime (such as a theft, assault, battery, etc.).

CRIMES

50 *'most charged'* crimes defined

CARJACKING

Taking a motor vehicle from the custody of another person by force, violence or assault or putting in fear.

The taking must be with the intent to temporarily or permanently deprive the victim of their right to use or possess the motor vehicle.

CRIMES

CHILD ABUSE

The intentional infliction of physical or mental injury, upon a child.

Or, any intentional act that could reasonably be expected to result in physical or mental injury to a child.

Anyone who actively encourages another to commit an act of child abuse is guilty of child abuse.

A child is a person under the age of 18.

CRIMES

CHILD PORNOGRAPHY

Possession of any image depicting a minor engaged in sexual conduct.

In most states each image is an additional count. Ten photos (electronic images) can become ten individual counts of child pornography.

CRIMES
50 *'most charged'* crimes defined

CONSPIRACY

A "conspiracy" is an agreement or a kind of "partnership" in criminal purposes in which each member becomes the agent or partner of every other member.

The essence of a conspiracy offense is the making of the agreement itself (followed by the commission of any overt act). It is not necessary for the Government to prove that the conspirators actually succeeded in accomplishing their unlawful plan.

The state must prove:

1. That two or more persons came to an understanding to do a criminal act.
2. That the defendant knowing the purpose willfully joined in.
3. That any of the conspirators made an overt act to advance the object of the conspiracy.
4. That the overt act advanced was knowingly done to carry out or advance the object of the conspiracy.

COUNTERFEITING

It is a Federal crime for anyone to falsely make or counterfeit any United States Federal Reserve Notes (money, bonds, etc.).

The defendant can be found guilty of that offense only if all of the following facts are proved beyond a reasonable doubt:

1. The defendant made a counterfeit federal reserve note (money, bonds, etc.).
2. It was done willfully and with intent to defraud.

To act with "intent to defraud" means to act with the specific intent to deceive or cheat, ordinarily for the purpose of causing some financial loss to another or bringing about some financial gain to one's self.

It is not necessary, however, to prove that the United States or anyone else was in fact defrauded so long as it is established that the defendant acted "with intent to defraud".

CRIMES
50 'most charged' crimes defined

CRIMINAL MISCHIEF

Causing damage to the property of another, willfully and maliciously.

'Maliciously' means wrongfully, intentionally, without legal justification or excuse and with the knowledge that the injury or damage will or may be caused to another person or the property of another person.

'Willfully' means intentionally, knowingly, and purposefully.

CRUELTY TO ANIMALS

To be guilty the state must prove:

The defendant unnecessarily overloads, overdrives, torments, deprives of necessary sustenance or shelter, or unnecessarily mutilates, or kills any animal, or causes the same to be done, or carries in or upon any vehicle, or otherwise, any animal in a cruel or inhumane manner.

It can be a felony if the defendant intentionally commits an act to any animal which results in the cruel death, or excessive or repeated infliction of unnecessary pain or suffering.

CRIMES

50 *'most charged'* crimes defined

DEALING IN STOLEN PROPERTY

Initiating, organizing, planning, financing, directing, managing or supervising the theft of property and trafficking in that property.

DELIVERY OR SALE OF
A CONTROLLED SUBSTANCE

'Delivery' or 'sale' means the actual, constructive, or attempted transfer from one person to another.

Money does not have to be exchanged. If you give it to someone for free it is considered delivery.

CRIMES

50 'most charged' crimes defined

DISORDERLY CONDUCT
BREACH OF THE PEACE

Acts which corrupt public morals or outrage the sense of public decency, affect the peace and quiet of persons who may witness them, brawling, fighting or breaches of the peace.

CRITICAL: CRIMES

CRIMES

50 *'most charged'* crimes defined

DRUG CRIMES

The state can prohibit entirely the use of particular drugs for which there is both a lawful and an unlawful market, and may exercise broad police powers in regulating the possession of drugs.

Controlled substances are divided into five categories, largely according to their relative potential for abuse.

It is a crime to be in possession of a controlled substance without a valid prescription.

CRITICAL

(DUI) DRIVING UNDER THE INFLUENCE

A person is guilty of Driving under the Influence if all the following can be proven by the state:

1. The defendant was in actual physical control of a vehicle (car, truck, motorcycle, bicycle, boat, motorbike).
2. The person was under the influence of alcohol, a chemical substance, a controlled substance; to the extent that one's normal faculties are impaired.
3. If the person has a blood alcohol level over the legal maximum (.08% in most states, 0.1 in a minority of states), you can be found guilty of DUBAL (driving with an unlawful blood alcohol level) or the law creates a rebuttable presumption of impairment.

Normal faculties include but are not limited to the ability to see, hear, walk, talk, judge distances, drive an automobile, make judgments, act in emergencies and, in general, to normally perform the many mental and physical acts of our daily lives.

Actual physical control means physically in or on the vehicle and has the capability to operate the vehicle, regardless of whether you are actually operating the vehicle at the time.

CRIMES

50 *'most charged'* crimes defined

FALSE IMPRISONMENT

Forcibly or secretly or by threat confining, abducting, imprisoning, or restraining a victim against his/her will without lawful authority.

CRITICAL

CRIMES

50 'most charged' crimes defined

FLEEING OR ELUDING (Vehicular)

The state must prove that the defendant:

1. Willfully refused or failed to stop.
2. The officer had police insignia on his vehicle.
3. Defendant was operating a vehicle.
4. A duly authorized law enforcement officer ordered the defendant to stop or remain stopped.
5. Defendant knew he had been directed to stop.

CRIMES

FORGERY

Falsely making or altering or counterfeiting a document with the intent to injure or defraud a person or a firm.

CRIMES
50 'most charged' crimes defined

GAMBLING

To prove the crime of gambling the state must prove that the defendant organized, participated or assisted in a game of chance in which the participant risks money or property on the outcome with the expectation of gaining or losing as a result of the game.

HOME INVASION ROBBERY

The state must prove:

1. The defendant entered the dwelling of the victim.
2. At the time the defendant entered the dwelling he (or she) intended to commit robbery.
3. While inside the dwelling the defendant committed a robbery.

CRIMES

50 *'most charged'* crimes defined

IDENTITY THEFT

The willful and unauthorized fraudulent use of personal identification or information about an individual, without first obtaining consent.

IMPROPER EXHIBITION OF A WEAPON

Elements:

1. Defendant had or carried a weapon.
2. The weapon was exhibited in a rude, careless, angry or threatening manner.
3. It was done so in the presence of one or more persons.

CRIMES

50 'most charged' crimes defined

KIDNAPPING

To prove the crime of kidnapping, the state must prove the following three elements:

1. Defendant forcibly, secretly, or by threat: confined, or abducted, or imprisoned the victim against his or her will.
2. The defendant had no lawful authority.
3. The defendant acted with intent to do any of the following:
   a. commit a felony
   b. hold for ransom
   c. inflict bodily harm
   d. terrorize the victim
   e. interfere with the performance of any governmental or political function.

LEAVING THE SCENE OF AN ACCIDENT

To prove the crime of leaving the scene of an accident the state must prove:

1. Defendant was the driver of a vehicle involved in an accident resulting in property damage, (usually means over $100.00) injury (or death) to any person.
2. Defendant knew, or should have known, that he/she was involved in an accident.
3. Defendant knew or should have known, of the damage, injury or death.
4. Defendant willfully failed to stop at the scene of the accident, or as close to the accident as possible, and remain there until he/she had given identifying information to the other driver, injured person, or police.
5. Defendant willfully failed to render reasonable assistance to the inured. This means not taking steps to aid the person or minimize the amount of damage.

CRIMES
50 *'most charged'* crimes defined

LEWDNESS

Any act which is wicked, lustful, unchaste, licentious, or sensual by intent.

LOITERING and PROWLING

To prove the crime of loitering and prowling, the state must prove:

1. Defendant loitered or prowled in a place, at a time, or in a manner not usual for law abiding individuals.
2. The loitering and prowling was under circumstances that warranted justifiable and reasonable alarm or immediate concern for the safety of persons or property in the vicinity.

To loiter is to linger or dawdle or remain or move about without a lawful purpose.

CRIMES

50 *'most charged'* crimes defined

MANSLAUGHTER

Manslaughter is killing a human being without malice, and without premeditation, and without justification or legal excuse. It is taking a human life by culpable negligence, but without the specific intent to cause death.

Manslaughter differs from murder: malice (evil intent) and premeditation is the essence of murder. Culpable negligence or the unintended causing of death is manslaughter.

Culpable negligence: Everyone has a duty to act reasonably towards others. If there is a violation of that duty, without any conscious intention to harm, that violation is negligence. But culpable negligence is more than failure to use ordinary care toward others. In order for negligence to be culpable, it must be gross and flagrant. Culpable negligence is a course of conduct showing reckless disregard of human life, or the safety of persons exposed to dangerous effects.

CRIMES
50 'most charged' crimes defined

MONEY LAUNDERING

A Defendant can be found guilty of this offense only if all of the following are proved beyond a reasonable doubt;

1. The defendant knowingly engaged, or attempted, to engage in a monetary transaction.
2. The defendant knew the transaction involved criminally derived property.
3. More than $10,000.00 was involved (federal).
4. The property was, in fact, derived from an unlawful activity, which must be proven.
5. The transaction occurred in the United States.

The term "monetary transaction" means the [deposit] [withdrawal] [transfer] or [exchange], in or affecting interstate commerce, of funds or a monetary instrument by, through, or to a financial institution obtained by *some* criminal offense.

CRIMES

MURDER

The unlawful and premeditated killing of a human being.

Killing with premeditation is killing after consciously deciding to do so.

The decision must be present in the mind at the time of the killing.

The law does not fix the exact period of time that must pass between the formation of the premeditated intent to kill and the killing.

The period of time must be long enough to allow reflection by the defendant. The premeditated intent to kill must be formed before the killing.

CRIMES
50 *'most charged'* crimes defined

OBSTRUCTION OF JUSTICE

Resisting, obstructing, or opposing any officer in the execution of any legal duty.

The crime of Obstructing Justice includes
Contempt
Escape
Perjury
Resisting or Obstructing an Officer
Retaliation against a witness
Tampering or fabricating evidence
Tampering with witnesses

CRITICAL:

CRIMES

50 *'most charged'* crimes defined

PERJURY

To prove Perjury the following elements must be proven:

1. The person took an oath to tell the truth.
2. While under oath the person made a false statement that he/she DID NOT believe to be true.

Perjury can also occur by contradictory statements, as follows:

While under oath a person made statements which are contradictory. Both statements were made knowingly and intentionally.

POSSESSION OF A CONTROLLED SUBSTANCE

'Possession' means to have personal charge of, or exercise the right of ownership, management, or control over the thing possessed.

Possession may be actual or constructive.

'Constructive possession' means the thing is in a place over which the person has control, or in which the person has concealed it.

If a person has exclusive possession of a thing, knowledge of its presence may be inferred or assumed.

CRITICAL: *CRIMES*

POSSESSION OF DRUG PARAPHERNAILA

The state must prove:

1. Defendant used or had the object in his/her possession with the intent to use it as drug paraphernalia.
2. Defendant had knowledge of the presence of the drug paraphernalia.

'Paraphernalia' means all equipment, products, and materials of any kind which are used, intended for use, or designed to use in planting, propagating, cultivating, growing, harvesting, manufacturing, compounding, converting, producing, processing, preparing, testing, analyzing, packaging, repackaging, storing, containing, concealing, injecting, ingesting, inhaling, or otherwise introducing into the human body a controlled substance.

CRIMES

50 *'most charged'* crimes defined

PROSTITUTION

The giving or receiving of the body for sexual intercourse, or any sex act, for hire.

CRIMES
50 *'most charged'* crimes defined

RECKLESS DRIVING

To prove reckless driving the state must prove two elements:

1. Defendant operated a vehicle.
2. Defendant did so with a willful or wanton disregard for the
    safety of persons or property.

Willful means intentionally, knowingly and purposely.

Wanton means with a conscious and intentional indifference to consequences and with knowledge that damage or injury is likely to result from the driver's actions.

CRIMES
50 *'most charged'* crimes defined

RESISTING AN OFFICER WITH VIOLENCE

The wrongful, knowing and willful obstruction or opposition by violence of a lawful act by a police officer.

CRIMES
50 'most charged' crimes defined

RETAIL THEFT

Knowing and intentional taking of retail merchandise with the fully formed intent to permanently (or temporarily) deprive the merchant of possession of or benefit of the retail merchandise.

CRIMES

50 *'most charged'* crimes defined

R.I.C.O.
(Racketeering Influenced and Corrupt Organization Act)

There are five specific facts which must be proved:

1. The defendant was associated with an "enterprise".
2. The defendant knowingly and willfully committed, or aided, at least two predicate offenses.
3. That the two predicate offenses were connected with each other by some common scheme, plan or motive, so as to be a pattern of criminal activity.
4. The defendant conducted or participated in the enterprises' affairs.

CRIMES
50 'most charged' crimes defined

ROBBERY

Four elements must be proven:

1. Defendant took money, or property, from the person or custody of the person.
2. Force, violence, assault, or putting in fear was used during the course of the taking
3. The property taken was of some value.
4. The taking was with the intent to permanently or temporarily deprive the victim of the property taken.

CRIMES

50 'most charged' crimes defined

SEXUAL BATTERY (RAPE)

An act by which the perpetrator's sexual organ, finger, hand or any object penetrates or has union with the anus, vagina or mouth of the victim.

Union means contact.

It requires a lack of consent on the part of the victim. Minors (under 18) cannot consent to any sex act.

CRIMES

STALKING

A course of conduct where the defendant willfully, maliciously and repeatedly followed or harassed the victim.

Harass means a course of conduct directed at a specific person that causes substantial emotional distress and serves no legitimate purpose.

Aggravated Stalking includes the added act of a credible threat that places the victim in reasonable fear of death or bodily injury.

A credible threat means a threat made with the intent to cause reasonable fear for one's safety, and must be against the life of the victim or a threat to cause bodily injury.

CRIMES

THEFT

To prove the crime of theft the state must prove:

1. Defendant knowingly and unlawfully obtained, used, or endeavored to use or obtain the property of another.
2. Defendant intended to either temporarily or permanently deprive the owner of the right to use, own, or benefit from the property.

CRIMES

50 *'most charged'* crimes defined

TRAFFICKING IN ILLEGAL DRUGS

To prove this the state must prove all of the following:

1. The defendant knowingly sold, purchased, manufactured, delivered, or possessed
2. A controlled substance (or a mixture containing a controlled substance)
3. The weight of which is more than 5 grams (Federal) most States' trafficking charges start at 28 grams for 'controlled substances'. Trafficking in some pills can be as few as ONE pill!
4. Knowing the substance or mixture contained a controlled substance
5. With the intention to sell, purchase, manufacture or deliver the controlled substance.

The State does not have to prove a sale. Giving drugs (at a party for example) is trafficking for some pills.

TRESPASSING

The elements of this crime are:

1. A willful entering or remaining in a structure, conveyance or land.
2. The structure, conveyance or land belonged to someone else. (Not the defendant).
3. The entering was without permission

'Willful' means intentionally and purposefully.

CRIMES

VEHICULAR HOMICIDE

The state must prove more than a failure to use ordinary care. The state must prove:

1. The victim is dead.
2. The death was caused by a motor vehicle operated by the defendant.
3. The defendant operated the motor vehicle in a reckless manner likely to cause death or great bodily injury.

The state does not have to prove any intent on the driver to injure the victim, just reckless operation.

CRIMES

50 *'most charged'* crimes defined

WITNESS TAMPERING

Knowingly using intimidation or physical force, threats, misleading conduct, or offers of money meant to influence the testimony of a witness.

CARS AND COPS

100 '*most asked* 'questions

CHAPTER SYLLABUS:

SEARCH AND SEIZURE

4TH AMNEDMENT

6TH AMNEDMENT

PRIVACY ISSUES

CARS AND COPS

100 'most asked' questions

CARS & COPS

CARS AND COPS

100 'most asked' questions

IF A PASSENGER HAS MARIJUANNA DO I GET ARRESTED?

Arrested, yes. Convicted?

To convict you of possession the state has to prove beyond a reasonable doubt that you had knowledge and actual or constructive control of a controlled substance.

You don't want the upfront experience of listening to lawyers argue over the fine distinctions between actual or constructive control, dominion, reach, knowledge.

You're certainly foolish, perhaps crazy, to remain in a vehicle when anyone in the car has a controlled substance. If a cop pulls the car over, your other passenger is almost certain to throw it under the seat, or on your lap, or out the window. Then it's anybody's game.

Do not ride in a vehicle if anyone in the vehicle has a controlled substance. They have to get out. If they don't get out of the car then you get out of the car. The End. No discussion.

SHOULD I "BLOW" IF I'M ARRESTED FOR DUI?

Most of my clients answer a resounding NO after their first arrest for DUI. Here's why...

Refusing the breath/alcohol test and roadside sobriety exam will expose you to harsher penalties....*if you are convicted.* In some states it's a misdemeanor to refuse to blow.

On the other hand, the state can, and will, use your breath and the video to convict you. By submitting to a breath test and a roadside sobriety examination you are providing evidence which will be used to convict you.

The state cannot convict you without evidence. The breath results and the video are almost always enough to convict you.

CARS AND COPS

100 *'most asked'* questions

WHEN IS A BORROWED CAR A STOLEN CAR?

Answer: when the owner says so.

If the rental car is overdue the rental company makes a call to the police and tells them it's stolen. A rental car kept beyond the term of your rental agreement becomes a stolen car. Congratulations, you are now driving a stolen car.

If your girlfriend, neighbor, friend, or family member wants the car back and calls the police and declares it stolen.......Bingo.... you now are driving a stolen vehicle.

Avoid this problem by respecting the owner's wishes and keep in regular contact with the owner. Call the rental car company if you need to extend the agreed return date.

CARS AND COPS

100 *'most asked'* questions

IF I'M DRIVING DO I HAVE TO STOP?

Yes.

If a cop signals you to pull over, pull over.

Failure to stop is a big mistake.

At the least you can be charged with a misdemeanor, resisting arrest without violence.

At worse aggravated fleeing.

Once the officer turns his siren on and activates his overhead lights it becomes a felony. If the cop follows you at a high rate of speed it becomes aggravated fleeing usually with a minimum mandatory prison sentence.

Some cops will set you up for prison by turning on their pursuit lights and cruising behind you. Don't confuse his lights with Christmas! It's an invitation to prison. Some cops play this game a lot, they win, and you lose.

CARS AND COPS

100 'most asked' questions

CAN THE POLICE SEARCH MY CAR AT A TRAFFIC STOP?

Yes.

The Supreme Court has given the police carte blanche to search your car if the stop is lawful.

The Supreme Court has gone so far as to say the police can search your car because you drove without your seat belt on.

They can search your car incident to arrest. They can search your car as an inventory search. They can search your car for a host of reasons.

The bottom line is this: if an officer has any legal reason to stop you, he can search your car. The days of expectations of privacy in an automobile are long gone.

The only chance you have of suppressing the search is if the stop itself was unlawful.

CARS AND COPS

CAN THE POLICE SEARCH MY CAR WITHOUT A WARRANT?

Yes.

If a police officer makes a lawful traffic stop he can search your car.

A lawful stop means the officer has at a minimum a reasonable belief that you have violated a criminal law, there is an outstanding warrant for the driver or passenger, or you committed a traffic infraction. The officer can detain you and your passengers for a reasonable time. Reasonable means a sufficient time to issue a citation for the infraction.

Everything within plain view, such as an open container of alcohol, a marijuana cigarette or a weapon can all give the officer probable cause to make an arrest of the driver and passengers.

The officer can detain the car, driver and the passengers for a reasonable time for a drug sniffing dog to be brought to the scene to alert to any controlled substance.

CARS AND COPS

100 'most asked' questions

CAN I GET A D.U.I. ON A BICYCLE?

Yes.

You can lose your drivers' license if you are riding a bicycle impaired.

Although a bicycle is not a motor powered vehicle, in most states the DUI statutes provide the same punishments for operating a motor vehicle or a bicycle while impaired.

If you're riding a bike without safety equipment, such as a working headlight to illuminate the road you can be stopped by an officer and issued a citation. Once you're stopped lawfully the officer can conduct a DUI investigation if he observes any indication of impairment.

CARS AND COPS

100 '*most asked* 'questions

CAN I GET A D.U.I. ON A BOAT?

Yes.

The penalty for operating a motor craft impaired is the same as operating a motor vehicle.

You can lose your drivers' license if you are operating your boat impaired.

DRUG BUSTS

100 *'most asked'* questions

Chapter Syllabus:

CONTROLLED SUBSTANCES

TRAFFICKING

POSSESSION CRIMES

DRUG BUSTS

100 'most asked' questions

DRUG BUSTS

DRUG BUSTS

100 'most asked' questions

WHAT IS POSSESSION?

To possess means to have personal charge of, or, exercise the right of ownership, management or control over the "thing" possessed.

Mere proximity to a thing does not prove possession. There has to be knowledge of its presence and control.

The law presumes you have knowledge of things within your control. That means anything on your person, in your clothing or within ready reach can be presumed to be in your possession.

You can be held accountable for possession of something that is not physically on your person. So, if you give a controlled substance to someone and it remains within your control, you can be charged with possession.

There are no easy rules or bright line distinctions between possession and mere proximity. It is always a question for the jury to decide.

IS RESIDUE POSSESSION?

Yes.

Residue *is* possession.

In most state courts they don't care if there is a trace amount, or a consumable amount of a controlled substance.

If it can be chemically identified as a controlled substance, or residue it is possession.

Ash is residue.

The film of smoke inside a pipe or bong is residue.

In most states you cannot be convicted of possession of a controlled substance if it is found in your body tissues or fluids.

Consuming a controlled substance, which often happens when someone is stopped by the police and tries to eat the drugs is charged as the crime of obstruction of justice, tampering with evidence, or resisting arrest.

DRUG BUSTS

100 'most asked' questions

WHAT IS CONSTRUCTIVE POSSESSION?

You can be charged with possession of a controlled substance under the constructive possession theory.

Constructive possession means that although the controlled substance is not on your person or within your immediate vicinity, the contraband is in a place over which you have control.

The state must prove: 1) control over the place 2) that you have actual knowledge it is there 3) that you can exercise dominion and exclude others from possession.

Constructive possession can be charged to one person or more than one person, if it can be proven that everyone had equal or shared possession, knowledge and control.

68

DRUG BUSTS

WHAT IS DELIVERY?

Transferring something.

If I give it to you it is a transfer (delivery).

You don't have to have an exchange of money to be guilty of delivery.

Giving a pill to a friend is delivery.

DRUG BUSTS

100 '*most asked* 'questions

WHAT IS TRAFFICKING?

Possession with the intent to sell or deliver any illegal drug (usually more than a personal use amount) or controlled substance is trafficking.

It commonly is understood to mean you have enough of the 'stuff' to be "in the business", and a transfer to someone. But, depending on what it is, and where you live, you can be a trafficker by giving away one pill.

Trafficking begins at 5 grams for federal law. Some States: 28 grams.

If you knowingly sell, buy, deliver (giving away a pill is a delivery) a controlled substance (anything illegal, anything that requires a prescription from a doctor), you can be convicted of trafficking.

Ever 'borrow' a sleeping pill? Pain medication? Give it to someone? Re-read the definition of trafficking: you are a trafficker. Scary stuff, huh?

(go to the appendix in this book for more information).

70

DRUG BUSTS
100 'most asked' questions

HOW MUCH IS A GRAM?

The penny in your pocket weighs 2.5 grams.

The nickel in your pocket weighs 5.0 grams.

Most states punish drug trafficking with a prison term of from 15 years to life.

DRUG BUSTS

100 'most asked' questions

MUST I KEEP IT IN THE PHARMACY CONTAINER?

Yes.

In most states you MUST keep and carry any prescription drug in the original container from the pharmacy.

If you have it on you (in your pocket or purse) or you transfer it into another container: it is a no-no.

CAN I SHARE MY PRESCRIPTION?

No.

The law makes no distinction between selling your prescription and giving away a single pill. If you transfer possession of a controlled substance to another person, you are guilty of sale or delivery.

Never offer to or share any pills with anyone. Never permit anyone else to carry your prescription for you. Never send your prescription ahead of you, if you're traveling and always keep it in the original container from the pharmacy.

If it can be proven that you gave someone a pill, or more than one pill from your prescription you can be charged with delivery or trafficking.

The person who receives it can be charged with possession, trafficking or conspiracy.

If the un-prescribed user were to overdose or have an allergic reaction you can be charged with a crime and sued for damages in civil court.

DRUG BUSTS

100 '*most asked* ' questions

IF MY ROOMATE HAS PARAPHERNALIA DO I GET ARRESTED?

Yes.

If you're in a place, or in a space, where a reasonable person can conclude that you are either in actual or constructive possession of paraphernalia you are subject to arrest.

This can be in a car, or in your dormitory room, or in your apartment.

The fact that the paraphernalia is in another room allows you grounds to argue; but not with a cop. Perhaps in front of the jury. Bad place to be.

If your roommate has paraphernalia either it/ he/she goes or you go.

CAN I BUY A BONG OR A PIPE?

Yes.

Can you possess it?

No.

This is a real head-scratcher for most of us.

A store can sell you what is obviously a device intended for the consumption of a controlled substance, but you can't possess paraphernalia.

It's a distinction without a difference to argue that it can be used for a non-controlled substance. That's not the issue. The only question is _can_ it be used to ingest a controlled substance.

If it can be used to consume a controlled substance it is a narcotic implement, also known as drug paraphernalia.

UNDER 21CROWD

100 '*most asked*' questions

Chapter Syllabus:

LEGAL MINORITY AND MAJORITY AGE ISSUES

CONTROLLED SUBSTANCES

PRIVACY ISSUES

ALCOHOL AND MINORS

SEARCH AND SEIZURE

ARREST AND DETENTION

UNDER 21CROWD

100 '*most asked* ' questions

FOR THE UNDER 21 CROWD

UNDER 21CROWD

IOO '*most asked* 'questions

IF I'M UNDERAGE AND ALCOHOL IS SERVED DO I GET ARRESTED?

Yes.

It is illegal for any person to sell, serve, or permit the serving of alcoholic beverages to a minor. The presence of alcoholic beverages and minors (under 21) in the same room gives rise to probable cause to make an arrest.

All the prosecutor has to prove is possession, either constructive, or actual.

The only exception is if you are under 21 and working in an establishment that serves alcohol: you can serve it.

CAN I CARRY ALCOHOL IN MY CAR?

No.

It is unlawful for an underage person to have alcohol in their possession.

The only exception is if you work in an establishment that serves alcohol. You can transport it only in connection with your work.

You do not want to have a discussion with the police about actual or constructive control of an alcoholic beverage. Nor do you want to be before a judge or the college administration.

Best not to carry alcohol in any form in your car.

It does not matter if the container is open or closed.

UNDER 21 CROWD

100 'most asked' questions

CAN SOMEONE UNDER 21 OWN ALCOHOL?

No.

Take a look at the definition of constructive possession and actual possession. If an under-age person has possession and control of alcohol, it is a crime.

If there is alcohol in your college dormitory room you can be arrested.

If there is alcohol in your apartment and you are under the legal drinking age you can be arrested.

DO I HAVE TO CARRY ID ON ME AT ALL TIMES?

No.

Should you? Yes.

Some states require that you identify yourself to law enforcement upon demand. It is important that you be able to identify yourself sometimes to protect yourself from arrest.

If police officer has a BOLO (be-on-look-out- for…) for a person of your general physical type and description, he can lawfully detain you and possibly arrest you if you cannot provide adequate identification.

Do not confuse your personal dignity and privacy rights with practical realities of the world.

Carrying identification with you at all times can be both a sword and a shield to protect you. Do not leave home without it.

WHAT'S THE LAW ON FAKE ID?

Possession of false ID is a crime.

It can be charged as a misdemeanor, or if you have a duplicate driver's license from another jurisdiction you can be charged with a felony.

Since '911' police agencies have a standard policy to arrest anyone with false or fake ID. After all you could be a terrorist. Right...

Using I.D. that belongs to another is possession of false I.D. Altered I.D. is false I.D.

CAN SOMEONE OVER 21 GIVE ME ALCOHOL?

No.

It is illegal for anyone to serve, give, sell or provide alcoholic beverages to anyone who is under the age of majority.

This law applies to parents, family members, friends or any other person of the same age, younger or older than the minor.

UNDER 21CROWD

100 'most asked' questions

CAN A "SECURITY GUARD" MAKE AN ARREST?

Yes.

Many states permit security guards to make arrests.

Many rent-a-cops are also off duty cops out there to pick up an extra dollar.

It is best to treat a rent-a- cop with the same concern as a police officer.   But it gets *worse*.

Rent-a-cops are not real cops, so you don't have constitutional rights if they violate your rights. That's a wow!

If a security guard tells you to stop: Stop.   Do not speak or explain.   You do not have any constitutional protections with a rent-a-cop.

Demand he release you or call a police officer. Be smart..... be safe..... be silent.

SEARCHES
100 'most asked' questions

CHAPTER SYLLABUS:

SEARCH AND SEIZURE

ARREST AND DETENTION

MIRANDA ISSUES

POLICE AGENTS

SCOPE OF SEARCHES

SEARCHES

100 'most asked' questions

SEARCHES

SEARCHES

100 'most asked' questions

SEARCHES

SEARCHES

CAN THE POLICE SEARCH ME?

They CAN search you ONLY if...

    1. You agree to the search.

Your consent must be freely and voluntarily given, and not the product of threats, intimidation, force, or the threatened use of force.

    2. For "Officer Safety"

They can search you for weapons only IF the officer has a good reason to believe you are a threat to his personal safety AND ONLY AFTER you are lawfully stopped or detained.

    3. After an arrest.

If a cop searches you without permission it is illegal, unless they have legal cause to search you. And that is for a judge to decide....later.

CAN THE POLICE ENTER MY HOUSE?

No.

Only with a warrant or "exigent" circumstances such as: they are chasing you, they get an emergency call that someone is being beaten or shot, a fire emergency.

You have a heightened expectation of privacy in your home. Therefore the police must get a search warrant before they can enter your home, or have a real good reason to tell the judge.

What is a home?

The law protects persons: not places. So what is in your mind is determinative.

Your home can be anywhere you feel like home: at a hotel room, as an overnight guest, in your room in a rooming house. It is always an open issue and an arguable question: like a snail who carries his home on his back: think home.

SEARCHES
100 'most asked' questions

HOW DO THE POLICE OBTAIN A SEARCH WARRANT?

To obtain a search warrant a police officer has to swear under oath, in a written affidavit, that he has probable cause to believe that the fruits or instrumentalities of a criminal act are in a certain place. He has to have evidence, not just a "hunch".

A search warrant closely defines where the police can go to seize the property and what the police can take.

SEARCHES
100 'most asked' questions

HOW DO I STOP A COP FROM SEARCHING ME?

Never agree to a search.

Always say no, even if it looks ridiculous at the time, you preserve your right to litigate the search.

Never resist with violence or force an officer who insists on searching.

A judge will suppress anything obtained by the police if the search was unlawful.

SEARCHES

100 'most asked' questions

WHAT IS A STOP & FRISK?

A cop can detain and ("stop") and pat down ("frisk") if he has:

    1. a "reasonable" suspicion of criminal behavior and/or

    2. "reasonable" concern for officer safety. This applies on the street and at a traffic stop.

The officer needs to have more than a "hunch", or a judge will throw out the search.

The officer needs to have something he can put into words which is both reasonable and rational….like "furtive movements" and reaching into bulky over-sized clothing, or a bulge that has the outline of a gun or knife.

He can't go rooting around in your pockets without 1 and 2.

SEARCHES
100 'most asked' questions

WHAT IS A STOP?

A "stop" is what comes before an arrest.

An officer who encounters any person under circumstances which reasonably indicate that such a person has committed or was about to commit a crime can temporarily stop that person.

If the stop is longer than reasonable then it is a detention. Being stopped "briefly" and being detained "longer" has constitutional implications.

SEARCHES

100 'most asked' questions

CAN THE POLICE LOOK INTO MY YARD?

Yes.

The police can look into your yard with binoculars, from airplanes, from a neighbor's yard, from anywhere.

If an officer is lawfully in a place from which he can view your home or yard it is with the Plainview exception to the search warrant requirement.

Looking into your yard can also mean examining your trash if it is put out for trash pickup.

You do not have any expectation of privacy in any garbage which is placed in a garbage container and left for pick up. That means your trash can be pulled and examined by police.

CAN THE POLICE WALK INTO MY YARD?

No.

They can if they have a warrant, are in "hot pursuit" or "exigent" circumstances exist.

'Exigent' means a real emergency.

The law requires the police to obtain a search warrant from an impartial Magistrate before they can enter your home.

If the police do not have a search warrant when entering your property and there is no lawful exception to permit an entry; any evidence of the crime and the evidence obtained as a direct result of the unlawful entry by the police can be suppressed.

HOW DO YOU SAY NO TO THE POLICE?

Just say no.

If you can say no to an insurance salesman who is trying to sell you insurance, you can say no to a cop: he is trying to sell you a prison term.

The police are an instrument of the State, not your mother or your priest.

The street is not the place to object to police actions, assert your rights, and seek fairness or justice.   That is what goes on in a court.

Just say no and call your lawyer from jail.

Loose lips sink ships.

CAN MY BOSS LOOK IN MY DESK?

Yes.

You do not have any expectation of privacy in a desk that belongs to your employer and is provided for your work.

Do not keep anything in your work space that you don't want others to find.

Constitutional rights only apply if the search is made by a police officer or someone acting as an agent of the police.

CAN MY BOSS LISTEN TO MY PHONE CALLS?

Yes.

Do not say or do anything on your employer's telephone that you don't want him to hear. They can listen and record and give it to the police.

You have no constitutional rights if your boss or his "security" department is listening on the office phone.

SEARCHES

100 'most asked' questions

CAN A TEACHER SEARCH A STUDENT'S LOCKER?

Yes.

That includes work lockers, gym lockers (even at your private club), dorm rooms, etc.

Places and spaces belonging to others and provided for your use have no constitutional protections for you.

Consider them as places that the police can search without your permission and without your knowledge at any time.

SEARCHES

CAN THE POLICE SEARCH ME ON SOMEONE'S LIE?

Yes.

It happens all the time. Someone angry with you calls the police and piles on a heap of lies. The police can search and arrest you based on someone's lies.

What can you do?

If the police act on a "confidential informant" or a "citizen informant" the search is subject to suppression if the search does not meet legal standards.

If the search is unlawful it will be thrown out.

The test is:

1. basis of the informant's knowledge
2. veracity
3. credibility
4. reliability
5. the totality of the circumstances.

WHAT IS PLAIN VIEW?

If a cop is in a place where "he has a right to be" it is not a search, it is "plain view".

If it is not a search then it is not subject to being suppressed.

The law protects your reasonable expectation of privacy. The reasonable test goes to expectations of privacy, not places.

Looking into cars is permitted. Using a flashlight to see in your car or your home is permitted. Binoculars: ok. Fly-over's: ok. And our courts keep expanding the list of permitted views.

Anything that can be seen from the street is in 'plain view' and you have no constitutional protection.

POLICE CONTACT

100 'most asked' questions

POLICE CONTACT

POLICE CONTACT

100 *'most asked'* questions

POLICE CONTACT

POLICE CONTACT

100 'most asked' questions

DO I HAVE TO TALK TO THE POLICE?

No.

You do not have to say anything to an officer to assist him in making a case against you.

The police can stop you in the street and talk to you. You do not have to, and should not, answer.

The only person who can force you to answer questions is a judge, and then only in limited circumstances. Those circumstances only occur in a courtroom. The street is not a courtroom. A cop is not a judge.

POLICE CONTACT

100 'most asked' questions

CAN I TRY TO MAKE A DEAL WITH THE POLICE?

No.

No police officer can make a deal. They do not have the legal power to make you a deal or cut you a break.

ONLY a prosecutor can negotiate and make an enforceable promise of leniency in return for assistance.

Don't even think about negotiating deals with cops.

If a prosecutor is standing next to the cop, ignore the cop, talk to the prosecutor.

POLICE CONTACT

100 'most asked' questions

CAN THE POLICE STOP ME ON THE STREET?

Yes.

They can stop you.

But you don't have to talk to them.

If you were "stopped" in the street by an insurance salesman you would walk away. The only thing a cop is selling is jail. Don't buy it.

Think this way...

If you have nothing to hide, you have nothing to prove.

If you have something to hide, you do not have to volunteer information that can be used to convict you.

POLICE CONTACT

100 '*most asked* 'questions

WHY IS THE COP TALKING TO ME?

9 times out of 10 he's talking to you because he needs something more from you to make a valid arrest.

The police cruiser may have "*TO SERVE AND PROTECT*" printed on the door, but that's not the truth. The police are there "*TO INVESTIGAGE AND ARREST*".

They are not there to protect your rights. That's what a lawyer is for.

If a police officer is talking to you assume he is conducting an investigation. DO NOT cooperate in a police investigation if you are the person of interest.

You cannot know what is in the mind of the police officer. You can only assume he is conducting an investigation with the objective of making an arrest. It is naïve to assume anything else.

POLICE CONTACT

100 'most asked' questions

CAN I WALK AWAY FROM A POLICE OFFICER?

Yes.

If a officer approaches you and engages you, simply ask "Am I free to go?"

If he says yes, then go.

If he says you are not free to go then, consider yourself stopped, detained and soon to be arrested. Exercise your right to remain silent.

If he has a reason to detain you he must issue a command for you to stop. If he does then you must stop, but you do not have to speak.

POLICE CONTACT

IS IT A CRIME TO REFUSE TO GIVE INFORMATION?

No.

If the police are conducting a criminal investigation and you are the 'person of interest' it is not a violation of law to withhold information that can incriminate you.

If there is any concern in your mind that you may somehow be drawn into their investigation and become a "person of interest" then refuse to answer any questions.

Demand the right to have an attorney present at any questioning.

If you have nothing to hide then you have nothing you need to tell the police.

POLICE CONTACT

100 '*most asked* 'questions

CAN I REFUSE TO GIVE A COP MY NAME?

Yes.

But some states have "stop and identify" laws which require you to give your name.

The general rule is as follows: It is not a crime to give a false name to an officer during a "consensual field interview": i.e. you are not under arrest. After an arrest it is a crime to give a false name.

POLICE CONTACT

DO I HAVE TO TELL THEM WHAT I KNOW?

No.

The only time you have to speak is if you are ordered to do so by a judge, in court, with your attorney present.

Once you begin to tell the police what you know you expose yourself to criminal charges of obstruction of justice, impeding a police investigation, filing a false police report, perjury, and a host of other criminal charges.

By remaining silent you are not exposing yourself to criminal liability for misstating or mistaking what you know from what you think you know.

You need to speak with a lawyer. You can cooperate in an investigation later if you want.

POLICE CONTACT
IOO '*most asked* 'questions

AM I OBSTRUCTING JUSTICE BY NOT ANSWERING?

No.

By refusing to answer the police officer's questions you have not obstructed justice. You cannot be arrested for refusing to answer a question.

You can, however, be prosecuted for making a false statement; don't put yourself in that position.

WHAT SHOULD I DO IF I AM BEING QUESTIONED BY THE POLICE?

Do not answer questions, do not volunteer.

Tell the police that you will not answer any questions without an attorney present.

It is the most natural thing in the world to try to defend yourself when you're being accused of a crime. And that's okay, and that's how it should be.

The thing to remember is time and place.

The time of your arrest, it is not the place to defend yourself. You cannot talk the police out of arresting you.

The correct time and place is in a courtroom.

POLICE CONTACT

100 '*most asked*' questions

CAN I TALK A COP INTO NOT ARRESTING ME?

No.

You cannot charm a cop into letting you go if he has legal reason to arrest you. You cannot negotiate with the police.

If a police officer has probable cause to arrest he must arrest you.

If they ask you to help them arrest someone else and in return they say they will let you go, do not believe it for one minute. Only a prosecutor can make that deal.

IS A RENT-A-COP A REAL COP?

No.

"Rent-a-cops", unless they are off duty police or have special statutory powers, do not have the legal authority to make an arrest, other than a "citizen's arrest".

If a rent-a-cop talks to you DO NOT answer and DO NOT respond. Tell them to get a real cop and then wait. Remain silent at all times! You have NO constitutional protections (i.e. Miranda rights), and no search and seizure protections from rent-a-cops. Private security officers often are used to defeat your constitutional protections: it is a mean-spirited end-run around the constitution.

POLICE CONTACT

SHOULD I OPEN THE DOOR
IF THE POLICE KNOCK?

Only if they have a warrant.

If they don't have a warrant and force their way in, then let a judge sort it out.

If they are in, just remain silent and comply with any command (sit still) .

Do not give them permission to search, even if the situation looks hopeless.

Remember that a lawful search is only admissible if:
   a) you give them permission,
   b) the police have a warrant,
   c) "exigent circumstances" exist.

To preserve the issue for a judge NEVER agree to a search.

POLICE CONTACT

100 'most asked' questions

CAN I ASK AN UNDERCOVER COP IF HE'S A COP?

Yes.

You can ask, but he doesn't have to tell you the truth.

WHAT IF I RUN?

Running away can be considered as an indication of guilt.

If an officer issues a command for you to stop you must do so. You do not have to cooperate or assist the officer in obtaining information which can lawfully empower him to arrest you.

If an officer commands you to stop you can consider yourself detained. All of your constitutional rights attach to the circumstances and subsequent actions of the officer. That means anything that happens after the issuance of the "stop" command by the officer is subject to review by a judge.

So if the officer says stop: stop. At that point exercise your right to remain silent and your right to counsel.

You gain control of the situation when you follow the law. Running is always an unwise response.

Remember the law can protect you if you know the law.

CAN THE POLICE LIE TO ME?

Yes.

The Supreme Court has said it is okay for the police to lie to you in the course of an investigation. That's a big WOW isn't it?

Does that mean the police can lie to me when they tell me that they have a confession from someone else and I've been implicated? Yes.

Does that mean the police can lie if they tell me they have a picture of me in a compromising criminal act? Yes.

Does that mean the police can lie if they tell me they have my fingerprints? Yes.

Gee, my Mom never lied to me like that.

The police are not your mother.

ARRESTS
100 *'most asked'* questions

CHAPTER SYLLABUS:

SEARCH AND SEIZURE

JUDICIAL ACTS

MIRANDA ISSUES

4TH AMENDMENT

6TH AMENDMENT

ARRESTS

100 '*most asked*' questions

ARRESTS

ARRESTS

100 *'most asked'* questions

WHAT IS AN ARREST?

Most people think they are arrested when a police officer says "You are under arrest" and puts you in the back of the police cruiser. Wrong.

An arrest is the act of legal authority taking actual physical custody of a citizen and is a restraint on that citizen's liberty. An arrest has occurred when there is a submission to authority. It is a seizure of your person. You are not free to go.

Understand that an arrest is more than a stop. It is more than a detention. Interaction with the police is not an arrest, it is contact.

The constitutional rights that most people know of as Miranda rights don't become real until after you are placed under arrest.

ARRESTS

DO THE POLICE NEED A WARRANT TO ARREST ME?

No.

The police do not need a warrant to place you under arrest.

If the police officer has probable cause to believe that a crime has been committed, you can consider yourself a candidate to be arrested.

ARRESTS

100 'most asked' questions

CAN I ASK A COP IF I'M UNDER ARREST?

Yes.

But the cop will avoid an answer.

They will dodge this question as long as possible.

If the officer was trying to entice you to make a voluntary statement you just put him on notice that it's time to fish or cut bait. And if you are being baited it's best to know that before you start telling a police officer everything he needs to arrest you.

All this sounds very mean spirited and cynical. It is neither, it is good advice

Believing for one moment you can talk a cop out of arresting you makes as much sense as giving a Burger King coupon to a raptor.

IS ANY POLICE CONTACT AN ARREST?

Consider any contact you have with the police a prelude to an arrest.

Like a foreword to a book, or an overture to a Broadway show: if you are talking to the police, consider yourself on a slippery slope to an arrest.

The police will often play a game of cat and mouse with someone who they want to interrogate. They know the difference between lawful contact, detaining a person and arresting a person.

The police know that anything you say before an arrest can be used against you. It is considered a voluntary statement.

If an officer is talking to you, your wisest course of action is to exercise your right to remain silent, and remain silent.

ARRESTS
100 'most asked' questions

CAN I BE ARRESTED FOR SOMETHING MY CHILD DID?

Yes.

Most states have imposed Parental Responsibility statutes.

That means a parent can be arrested and prosecuted for a criminal act committed by their child.

That is a major WOW!

The law states that a parent has the duty to supervise and control the acts of their child.

Obviously, these laws were written by legislators who do not have children.

100 *'most asked'* questions

WHEN CAN A COP ARREST ME?

A police officer can only make a lawful arrest if he has probable cause, or a warrant.

The police make unlawful arrests all the time, and the cases get thrown out.

It makes good sense to remember the mantra; *contact, stop, detention, arrest.*

Your constitutional rights only attach after an arrest. If you regard any contact with the police as an arrest and remember your constitutional rights you can protect yourself.

ARRESTS
IUU '*most asked*' questions

CAN I RELY ON LEGAL ADVICE FROM THE POLICE?

No.

Don't rely on the police to give you legal advice. You can depend on them giving you bad advice if any advice at all.

You need to speak to a lawyer.

ARRESTS

100 'most asked' questions

IF I'M ARRESTED DO THE POLICE HAVE TO READ ME MY RIGHTS?

No.

Miranda has nothing to do with the legality of the arrest.

Miranda concerns statements made **after** an arrest, not before.

If you make a statement to the police before the arrest, it is considered voluntary. A voluntary statement can be used in court.

ARRESTS
100 'most asked' questions

IF I AM WRONGLY ARRESTED CAN I RESIST?

No.

You must submit to an arrest. If the arrest is wrongful it will be a judge who decides that, not you.

The street is the wrong place to dispute an arrest. Just go along with the cop and your lawyer will straighten it out in court.

Resisting arrest is a serious crime. If you resist with violence you face a prison sentence in most states.

It is always a mistake to resist an arrest. Don't do it.

ARRESTS

100 'most asked' questions

WILL A JUDGE DISMISS MY CASE IF I WAS NOT GIVEN MY MIRANDA WARNINGS?

No.

Many people mistakenly believe that their case will be thrown out of court by a judge if the police failed to give Miranda warnings.

It is not necessary for the police to give you a Miranda warning before you are arrested.

131

ARRESTS
100 '*most asked*' questions

WHEN CAN I ASK FOR A LAWYER?

Anytime.

Your right to counsel, even if waived, is always yours to reclaim.

You can stop at anytime you are being interrogated: in mid-sentence, *anytime*.

ARRESTS
100 'most asked' questions

DOES MY RIGHT TO
REMAIN SILENT EVER END?

No.

It is always there, waiting for you.

If you begin a statement you can stop at any time and exercise your constitutional right to remain silent.

You can reclaim it at anytime.   It is never permanently waived.

BAIL
100 'most asked' questions

Chapter Syllabus:

BAIL

PRETRIAL RELEASE

CONFRONTATION CLAUSE

JUDICIAL ACTS

BAIL

100 'most asked' questions

BAIL

BAIL

WHAT IS BOND?
WHAT IS BAIL?

Bond is get-out-of- jail before trial money.

Bond is set by a judge. Bail is the amount of money required.

You have the right to some form of pre-trial release in most cases. There are two ways to get out of jail during the pre-trial period: ONE is Conditional Pre-Trial Release (no money but arduous conditions), TWO is bond (money).

If you miss court, get a new law violation, or violate any conditions of bond (set by the judge), the judge can put you in jail until the trial and you lose the bond money.

CAN I GET OUT WITHOUT MONEY?

Yes. It's called pre-trial release.

If you can convince the judge that you are not a risk of flight, that you don't present a danger to the community, and you are not a threat to the "victim"; then the judge can release you on pre-trial release.

Pre-Trial-Release (also known as Release On One's Own Recognizance or ROR) is usually given only on minor non-violent Misdemeanor cases and Misdemeanor drug charges.

The down-side of Pre-trial Release is the special conditions: Daily check-ins, phone monitoring, GPS monitoring, and many (any) other conditions the Judge and/or prosecutor can come up with.

BAIL

100 '*most asked*' questions

HOW DO I PAY FOR BOND?

Cash.

You can take the money to the bond window at the jail. If you post your own bond, you get it back when your case is resolved.

If you don't have enough money to post bond, you go to a bail bondsman.

The bondsman will require collateral.

WHO DECIDES HOW MUCH BOND I HAVE TO COME UP WITH?

The Judge.

Only a judge can set bond amount: you appear before a judge to get bond, set bond or get bond reduced.

Because in all cases (except life felonies) you have the right to bond, the law requires you be brought before a magistrate within 24 hours.   Most people have a bond hearing via a TV hookup from jail.

Bond hearings are held every day, seven days a week, 365 days a year.

BAIL
100 '*most asked*' questions

WHAT CAN I DO IF I CAN'T AFFORD TO POST BOND?

You stay in jail.

CAN I GET THE BOND REDUCED?

Yes.

It's called a bond reduction hearing. Your lawyer can get a bond reduction hearing if the initial bond is too high.

You are entitled to a "reasonable bond". Reasonable bond means reasonable for you, not an "average" or "normal" defendant.

At the hearing you have to convince the judge that you are not a risk of flight, have sufficient ties to the community to assure your appearance, not a danger to the community, and do not present continuing danger to the victim.

You only have one chance to reduce bond.

BAIL

100 '*most asked* 'questions

HOW SOON AFTER ARREST
DO I GET TO SEE THE JUDGE?

24 hours.

WHAT DOES A BONDSMAN CHARGE?

10%.

Most bondsman charge a 10% premium to "write" bond.

You have to sign over to the bondsman collateral equal to the bond amount AND pay the bondsman a fee of 10% of the bond amount.

They accept: houses, land, bank accounts. Most do not accept cars, motorcycles, jewelry.

Even if you can raise the cash I suggest you use a bondsman for this reason: Florida (and other states) will not return the money to you in full. The Clerk will take the court fines and other costs from your bond amount and then return the balance. No such risk for bondsmen.

If the Clerk doesn't take court costs and fines from the bond then it is cheaper for you to post the cash bond with the Sheriff. You get it all back at the end of the case (trial verdict or final disposition).

WHO DECIDES?

100 '*most asked* ' questions

Chapter Syllabus:

EXECUTIVE BRANCH POWERS

CONFRONTATION CLAUSE

WHO DECIDES?

100 'most asked' questions

WHO MAKES THE DECISION TO CHARGE SOMEONE WITH A CRIME?

WHO DECIDES?

WHAT DOES THE STATE ATTORNEY DO?

Prosecute.

District Attorney, State Attorney, Statewide Prosecutor's Office, U.S. Attorney, they all prosecute.

They do not arrest, the police do that. The prosecutor makes the decision on what charge to file by presenting their accusation to a grand jury, or by the filing of a document called the Prosecutor's Information.

The indictment or Prosecutor's Information, is the actual piece of paper that notifies you of which statute, what law, and what elements of proof, must be proven if the state seeks to convict you of a violation of criminal statute.

Every crime must be codified, that is, be in a written law. Criminal statutes laws are created by legislatures, not by judges.

WHO DECIDES?

CAN THE POLICE
CHARGE ME WITH A CRIME?

No.

The police can only investigate and arrest.

When they arrest you, the police will identify a criminal charge, but that is not and may not be the actual charge filed.

The prosecutor, not the police actually begin the process of bringing you before a judge and jury.

The actual charging document is called a 'Prosecutor's Information' or an 'Indictment'.

WHO DECIDES?

100 'most asked' questions

CAN A VICTIM CHARGE SOMEONE WITH A CRIME?

No.

The victim cannot charge you with a crime. Only the prosecutor's office can charge you.

The victim becomes the state's witness. The victim will testify at the trial.

CAN THE VICTIM STOP A PROSECUTION?

No.

The government is the moving party in any criminal prosecution. The victim is a witness.

The victim cannot begin and cannot end a prosecution.

WHO DECIDES?

WHAT STATE AGENCIES PROSECUTE?

The Police arrest.

The Prosecutor prosecutes.

The Judicial Branch determines if the evidence is sufficient to convict.   The judge sentences.

A police investigation is not a prosecution.

The State Attorney (also called District Attorney), a statewide prosecutor, or the Department of Justice (U.S.) prosecutes.

DISCOVERY

IOO '*most asked* 'questions

DISCOVERY

DISCOVERY
100 'most asked 'questions

HOW DO I GET TO SEE THE EVIDENCE?

Demand it.

Most states have what is called discovery rights. This means that your attorney, once he is on the case, can demand that the state permit him to view, inspect, and copy all the physical or testimonial evidence the state intends to use at trial. This also includes inspection of physical evidence such as weapons, contraband, and videotapes.

In federal court it's all upside down. In federal court you have very limited rights to see the evidence before trial. Most lawyers agree federal courts are leading the charge backward toward the Middle Ages; I call it the Dark Ages, of civil/criminal rights.

Most states have more and expanded discovery rights than are permitted in federal court.

CAN I KNOW THE WITNESSES' NAMES?

Yes.

Under the confrontation clause of the United States Constitution you have a right to know the names of your accusers.

As part of your discovery package the prosecutor will reveal to you the names of the witnesses the state intends to bring to testify at trial. States must also provide you with copies of their statements, and some states allow you to ask them questions by deposition.

DISCOVERY

CAN I SPEAK TO THE "VICTIM"?

Yes.

The victim is a witness and has no special status beyond that. You have the right to confront your accusers under the Constitution.

Your attorney alone can contact the victim. It is almost always ordered that the accused have no contact with the victim during the pendency of the criminal matter. This is both for the protection of the victim and to prevent any new accusations or acts of violence.

DISCOVERY

100 'most asked' questions

WHAT LAWYERS DO

A lawyer knows the law, is experienced in court, and knows the rules of evidence.

The lawyer will act to protect you at all stages of the criminal process. Do not try to represent yourself.

Seek and obtain legal counsel from the very beginning. The longer you wait the worse your chances of a good result.

A defendant who represents his or herself has a fool for a client.

DISCOVERY

100 *'most asked'* questions

WHAT IS A PRE-TRIAL MOTION?

Asking the judge to make a ruling on matters that are expected to come up at trial; before the jury is selected.

DISCOVERY

100 'most asked' questions

WHAT IS A DEPOSITION?

In deposition your lawyer gets to interrogate the governments' witnesses under oath, in a question and answer format before a court reporter.

The questions and answers are available for use at trial.

DISCOVERY

100 'most asked' questions

WHO PAYS FOR EXPERTS?

You.

Most criminal law attorneys do not include expert costs in the defense fees therefore; the client is responsible for expert witness fees.

DEFENSES
100 'most asked' questions

DEFENSES

DEFENSES

100 'most asked ' questions

WHAT IS A LEGAL DEFENSE?

A legal defense is a bar to a conviction. That is very different from being not guilty.

Entrapment, self defense, insanity, duress, these are legal defenses. In effect you are saying yes I did it but you can't convict me.

The problem with asserting a legal defense is that you have to admit your guilt and then prove your legal defense.

A legal defense is created by statute or by court rule.

160

ENTRAPMENT

Entrapment is a legal defense.

There are TWO forms of entrapment:

1. **Objective Entrapment** focuses on the conduct of law enforcement. It is a bar to prosecution when the government's conduct is so egregious and so offends decency or a sense of justice that it amounts to a denial of due process. (Examples: police offering sex in return for drugs or police cooking up crack in a police laboratory then selling it).

2. **Subjective Entrapment** focuses on an apparent lack of predisposition on the part of the defendant: when the police (or a police agent) present a criminal opportunity to a person who is not looking for it.

If there is no police involvement entrapment is not a defense.

DEFENSES
100 'most asked' questions

SELF DEFENSE

The Defendant, must have reasonably believed that his conduct was necessary to defend himself or another, against the imminent use of unlawful force by another person

AND:

    1. The use of unlawful force by the other person must have appeared to the defendant to be ready to take place.

    2. The defendant did not create the situation which necessitated his use of force to defend himself or another.

DEFENSES
100 '*most asked*' questions

INSANITY

If a person had a mental infirmity, disease, or defect and because of this condition he did not know what he was doing, or its consequences, or although he knew what he was doing and its consequences he did not know it was wrong: he is insane.

A defendant who believes that what he was doing was morally right is not insane if the defendant knew what he was doing violated societal standards or was against the law.

All persons are presumed to be the sane. The defendant has the burden of proving the defense of insanity by clear and convincing evidence.

DEFENSES

100 'most asked' questions

DURESS OR NECESSITY

It is a defense to a crime if the defendant acted out of duress or necessity.

That means all of the following have to be proven by the defendant:

1. The defendant reasonably believed a danger or emergency existed which was not intentionally caused by him.

2. The danger or emergency threatened significant harm to himself or third person.

3. The threatened harm was real, imminent and impending.

4. The defendant had no reasonable means to avoid the danger or emergency except by committing the crime.

The threat of a future harm is not sufficient to prove this defense.

INTOXICATION

Voluntary Intoxication may not be a defense where you live.   It is not a good defense in many states, having been eliminated by statute.

The use of alcohol or drugs to the extent that it merely arouses passions, diminishes perceptions, releases inhibitions, or clouds reason and judgment does not excuse the commission of a criminal act.

However, where a certain mental state is an essential element of a crime, and a person was so intoxicated that he/she was incapable of forming that mental state, the mental state would not exist and therefore the crime could not be committed.

Ask a lawyer licensed in your state about intoxication.

INVOLUNTARY INTOXICATION is a disfavored defense in most states and does not immunize a person from the consequences of criminal acts.   But, if the involuntary intoxication creates a state similar to insanity or unconscious acts it is a defense.

TRIAL
100 'most asked' questions

Chapter Syllabus:

CONFRONTATION CLAUSE

DUE PROCESS

EVIDENCE

JUDICIAL BRANCH POWERS

TRIAL

100 *'most asked'* questions

TRIAL

TRIAL
100 'most asked' questions

CAN I CHANGE JUDGES?

Yes.

It's called recusing a judge.

Judge shopping is not permitted.

In criminal courts judges are assigned to cases randomly. You cannot choose a judge: you can only ask a judge to step down.

The standard is whether the facts would place a reasonably prudent person in fear of not receiving a fair and impartial trial. It is a question of perception; it's not a question of fact.

Judges can be disqualified for communicating with either party privately, showing bias, prejudging someone, not appearing impartial, taking sides, helping either the defendant or the prosecutor by giving them tips or advice in court, or having the appearance of favoring one side over the other.

TRIAL

100 'most asked' questions

WHO PICKS THE JURY?

You cannot pick your jury. You can only remove jurors.

You're presented with the panel, usually 30 to 35 potential jurors. In federal court the judge asks questions. In state court your lawyer asks questions.

The questions relate only to the potential juror's ability to be fair and impartial.

You can remove some jurors (usually a maximum of 10) for what is called a peremptory challenge. That means you only have to explain the reason you're removing them if the other attorney suggests a racial or ethnic motive on your part.

You can remove an unlimited number of jurors for cause. That means you can rationally argue that they are unqualified to sit as a juror.

TRIAL

100 '*most asked*' questions

CAN I ASK QUESTIONS TO A WITNESS?

Yes.

You have the constitutional right to confront your accusers.

That means you have a constitutional right to compel witnesses to appear in court.

You can compel the government to tell you who the accusers are; and require they come to court to make the accusations in front of you and the jury.

There is no such thing as trial by affidavit, sworn statements, or any evidence which cannot be subject to cross-examination and challenge.

170

TRIAL

100 *'most asked'* questions

WHAT IS REASONABLE DOUBT?

Reasonable doubt is what the term defines: The doubt must be reasonable.

The government is not required to produce evidence that will exclude every possibility of innocence. It is only required to prove guilt with evidence beyond a reasonable doubt.

A reasonable doubt is a fair doubt, based upon reason and common sense.

Reasonable doubt can come from the evidence, the lack of evidence or conflict in the evidence.

TRIAL
100 'most asked' questions

WHAT ARE THE PARTS OF A TRIAL?

Pre – Trial Motions (Motion in Limine).

Jury selection.

Opening statements.

Prosecution's case.

Defense's case (optional).

Closing statements.

Jury instructions.

Jury deliberation and verdict.

DOES THE JURY FIND OUT ABOUT MY PAST?

No.

If you testify at your trial, yes... ....

but then the only thing they will hear is the number of felony convictions you have.

They will not be told what you were convicted of, only that you have been convicted and only if your convictions are for a felony, or any criminal charge that involves false swearing or dishonesty.

TRIAL
IOO 'most asked ' questions

CAN A CHILD BE A WITNESS?

Yes.

You can ask the judge to speak to the child before the child testifies. The judge's only concern is whether or not the child knows the difference between truth and a lie and understands the nature of an oath to tell the truth.

It is for the jury to decide how much weight to place upon the testimony of any witness.

100 'most asked' questions

CAN I FORCE SOMEONE TO TESTIFY?

Yes.

The judge must help you if you ask. The judge will issue a subpoena to compel the attendance of any witness you need.

No one can avoid attending a trial as a witness if they are served a subpoena.

If a witness ignores a subpoena the judge can order the police to pick them up and hold them in jail until the trial and then bring them out to testify.

CAN A GUILTY PERSON BE FOUND NOT GUILTY?

Yes.

If the government can't produce proof beyond a reasonable doubt of each and every element of a crime charged you cannot be convicted.

WHEN IS A GUILTY PERSON NOT GUILTY

When a jury says not guilty.

When a jury is convened to try a case they do not KNOW and cannot KNOW the truth. They can only hear the evidence and make a finding.

TRIAL
100 'most asked' questions

WHAT IS EVIDENCE?

Something legally presented before a court, such as a statement of a witness, an object or thing that bears on or establishes the point in question.

Evidence can be testimonial (spoken).
Evidence can be physical (a thing or object).

WHAT DOES MATERIAL MEAN?

'Material' means any subject, regardless of its admissibility under the rules of evidence, which could affect the course or outcome of the proceeding or the outcome of the case.

An element of a crime is material.

100 '*most asked*' questions

WHAT DOES RELEVANT MEAN?

Relevant evidence is evidence tending to prove or disprove a material fact.

NOTES

100 'most asked' questions

SENTENCING
100 *'most asked'* questions

Chapter Syllabus:

EXECUTIVE POWERS

LEGISLATIVE POWERS

EQUAL PROTECTION

DUE PROCESS

SENTENCING

100 'most asked' questions

SENTENCING

SENTENCING

100 'most asked' questions

DO I HAVE TO GO TO JAIL?

No.

Historically jail was the only sentence a court could impose.

Most states have created many alternative sentencing options.

Now there are mental health courts and mental health probation for people who suffer from mental diseases or disorders. Drug Courts exist to offer intervention programs with drug therapy for substance abusers.

A good lawyer can fashion many alternatives to jail or prison if your jurisdiction offers them.

SENTENCING

CAN I GET PROBATION?

Yes, if you don't score prison.

Probation is a sentence, which means the court has imposed a sanction. This is different from pretrial release, pretrial supervision/bond/bail.

Probation is an alternative to jail and the least onerous sanction a court can impose.

More restrictive sanctions than probation are: house arrest or community control, where you are under constant and regular supervision and your activities are limited to work and home.

While on probation you check-in once a week with your probation officer. You and your home are subject to random checks and searches. You have no constitutional rights to object to a search conducted by your probation officer.

As a general rule only 30% of those placed on probation successfully complete without a violation. Not all violations result in a prison sentence. Probation can be a slippery slope to prison: probation is more about compliance and submission to authority than punishment.

WHAT IS ADMINISTRATIVE PROBATION?

You check-in by mail.   No office visits required.

You already know that standard probation requires you to check in weekly with a probation officer. It requires you to reside in the community, maintain employment, maintain a regular address and phone number, and submit to probation searches.

If you have no prior criminal history and are regarded as a low risk person some states can offer you administrative probation: which is probation without supervision.

Administrative probation, also known as write-in probation, only requires that you file a monthly report. In the report you must affirm under oath that you had no contact with law enforcement, which means no new arrests. You also have to swear or affirm that you have complied with all the conditions of probation.

SENTENCING

100 *'most asked'* questions

WHAT IS PROBATION?

Probation is a sentence.

After your case has been resolved either by plea or trial: if you are adjudicated, the court must impose a lawful sentence.

A lawful sentence can be imprisonment, probation, community control (house arrest), or any combination of the above.

Probation means a form of community supervision requiring a weekly check in with a probation officer. You are subject to random searches of your home without notice and without a search warrant. Conditions of probation must be announced in court at your sentencing. Probation conditions vary from merely inconvenient to extremely inconvenient. They often include restrictions on consumption of alcohol, travel, and weekly reports at the probation office.

SENTENCING

WHAT IS DRUG OFFENDER PROBATION?

Intensive supervision which emphasizes treatment of drug offenders, with individualized treatment plans.

It is standard probation plus intensive supervision, and treatment for drug and substance abuse issues.

The emphasis is placed on rehabilitation and effective treatments assisting persons with substance abuse issues to help conquer them, often requiring intensive intervention, therapy, and rehabilitation.

Most states have special courts for first offenders charged with lesser drug crimes.

If a drug court is available in your jurisdiction it can be an excellent alternative to the traditional criminal courtroom.

In most states successful completion of drug offender sentences is rewarded with a dismissal of the underlying criminal charge. That means you will have no criminal record. This is a very important consideration. If a drug court program is available to you should discuss it with your attorney.

WHAT IS COMMUNITY CONTROL?

Your home is your jail.

You cannot leave your home without permission, unless you have a schedule which has been approved in advance by your community control officer.

Your activities are limited: you can be at work or at home. Any other activity is a violation and you are subject to being placed in jail or prison.

You will often be required to wear a GPS monitor on your ankle.

SENTENCING

100 'most asked' questions

WHAT IS SEX OFFENDER PROBATION?

"Sex offender probation" or "sex offender community control" means a form of intensive supervision, with or without electronic monitoring, which emphasizes treatment and supervision of a sex offender in accordance with an individualized treatment plan.

SENTENCING

WHO DECIDES ON THE SENTENCE?

The judge.

Juries do not sentence you. Only a judge can impose a sentence and only after a conviction by jury, or you plead guilty to the judge.

Judges cannot offer you a sentence. You cannot negotiate with the judge. The judge must first determine whether your guilt has been proven or if your plea of guilty is knowing and voluntary.

The judge is not your friend. The judge cannot help you. The judge cannot advise you. Do not think for a moment that the judge will be lenient because you are in a bad situation.

Think of the judge as an umpire. An umpire will not award the game to one team over another, he can't. He calls the strikes, calls the fouls, and is there to make sure the rules are followed.

Judges must follow the sentencing law in your jurisdiction. You cannot appeal a judge's sentence unless the sentence is illegal in some way. This rarely happens.

SENTENCING

CAN I APPEAL A SENTENCE?

Yes.

The grounds are very limited and appellate courts rarely reverse the trial court's sentence.

You can appeal a sentence that is unlawful. That means outside the legal range permitted either by statute or by the sentencing code, vindictive, lacks proportionality is cruel and unusual, was imposed without effective assistance of counsel or beyond the court's jurisdiction.

Very, very, few sentences are overturned by appellate courts. At best you can have the case sent back for re-sentencing.

SENTENCING

WHAT ARE THE SENTENCING GUIDELINES?

An arithmetical formula, that seeks to fairly balance the relationship between the length of the sentence, the seriousness of the crime and the offender's criminal history.

It assists the judge in imposing a rational sentence on all defendants regardless of race, gender, and economic status.

Crimes are organized by offense category, given an arithmetical value, and points are added reflecting the criminal history of each offender.

The total is a range within which a judge can lawfully sentence a convicted person.

Since the 1980's the U.S. federal system has used sentencing guidelines. Many states have created their own punishment code/sentencing guidelines.

If you score below the minimum prison sentence required by law you may be able to avail yourself of the many alternative sentences outlined above.

SENTENCING

100 *'most asked'* questions

ARE MINIMUM MANDATORY SENTENCES REAL?

Yes.

Since the mid 1980's legislatures across the country have been imposing minimum mandatory sentences.

Minimum mandatory sentences now exist for sexual offenders, battery on law-enforcement officers, drug related crimes such as drug trafficking and crimes in which a gun is used or displayed. Every year legislatures create more and more mandatory sentences and take sentencing options and authority away from judges.

A mandatory sentence cannot be ignored by a judge. Mandatory sentences are exactly that: minimum terms of incarceration.

APPENDIX

APPENDIX I

Federal Drug Trafficking Penalties

DRUG/ SCHEDULE	QUANTITY	PENALTIES	QUANTITY	PENALTIES
Cocaine (Schedule II)	500 - 4999 gms mixture	**First Offense**:Not less than 5 yrs, and not more than 40 yrs. If death or serious injury, not less than 20 or more than life. Fine of not more than $2 million if an individual, $5 million if not an individual	5 kgs or more mixture	**First Offense**: Not less than 10 yrs, and not more than life. If death or serious injury, not less than 20 or more than life. Fine of not more than $4 million if an individual, $10 million if not an individual. **Second Offense**: Not less than 20 yrs, and not more than life. If death or serious injury, life imprisonment. Fine of not more than $8 million if an individual, $20 million if not an individual.
Cocaine Base (Schedule II)	5-49 gms mixture		50 gms or more mixture	
Fentanyl (Schedule II)	40 - 399 gms mixture		400 gms or more mixture	
Fentanyl Analogue (Schedule I)	10 - 99 gms mixture		100 gms or more mixture	
Heroin (Schedule I)	100 - 999 gms mixture		1 kg or more mixture	
LSD (Schedule I)	1 - 9 gms mixture		10 gms or more mixture	
Methamphetamine (Schedule II)	5 - 49 gms pure or 50 - 499 gms mixture	**Second Offense**: Not less than 10 yrs, and not more than life. If death or serious injury, life imprisonment. Fine of not more than $4 million if an individual, $10 million if not an individual	50 gms or more pure or 500 gms or more mixture	**2 or More Prior Offenses:** Life imprisonment
PCP (Schedule II)	10 - 99 gms pure or 100 - 999 gms mixture		100 gm or more pure or 1 kg or more mixture	

Federal Drug Trafficking Penalties

PENALTIES

Other Schedule I & II drugs (and any drug product containing Gamma Hydroxybutyric Acid)	Any amount	**First Offense**: Not more that 20 yrs. If death or serious injury, not less than 20 yrs, or more than Life. Fine $1 million if an individual, $5 million if not an individual.
Flunitrazepam (Schedule IV)	1 gm or more	**Second Offense**: Not more than 30 yrs. If death or serious injury, not less than life. Fine $2 million if an individual, $10 million if not an individual
Other Schedule III drugs	Any amount	**First Offense**: Not more than 5 years. Fine not more than $250,000 if an individual, $1 million if not an individual.
Flunitrazepam (Schedule IV)	30 to 999 mgs	**Second Offense**: Not more 10 yrs. Fine not more than $500,000 if an individual, $2 million if not an individual
All other Schedule IV drugs	Any amount	**First Offense**: Not more than 3 years. Fine not more than $250,000 if an individual, $1 million if not an individual. **Second Offense**: Not more than 6 yrs. Fine not more than $500,000 if an individual, $2 million if not an individual.
Flunitrazepam (Schedule IV)	Less than 30 mgs	
All Schedule V drugs	Any amount	**First Offense:** Not more than 1 yr. Fine not more than $100,000 if an individual, $250,000 if not an individual. **Second Offense**: Not more than 2 yrs. Fine not more than $200,000 if an individual, $500,000 if not an individual.

Federal Trafficking Penalties – Marijuana

DRUG	QUANTITY	1st OFFENSE	2nd OFFENSE
Marijuana	1,000 kg or more mixture; or 1,000 or more plants	Not less than 10 years, not more than life If death or serious injury, not less than 20 years, not more than life Fine not more than $4 million if an individual, $10 million if other than an individual	Not less than 20 years, not more than life. If death or serious injury, mandatory life Fine not more than $8 million if an individual, $20 million if other than an individual
Marijuana	100 kg to 999 kg mixture; or 100 to 999 plants	Not less than 5 years, not more than 40 years.If death or serous injury, not less than 20 years, not more than life.Fine not more than $2 million if an individual, $5 million if other than an individual	Not less than 10 years, not more than life. If death or serious injury, mandatory life.Fine not more than $4 million if an individual, $10 million if other than an individual
Marijuana	more than 10 kgs hashish; 50 to 99 kg mixture more than 1 kg of hashish oil; 50 to 99 plants	Not more than 20 years If death or serious injury, not less than 20 years, not more than life. Fine $1 million if an individual, $5 million if other than an individual	Not more than 30 years. If death or seroius injury, mandatory life.Fine $2 million if an individual, $10 million if other than individual
Marijuana	1 to 49 plants; less than 50 kg mixture	Not more than 5 years Fine not more than $250,000, $1 million other than individual	Not more than 10 years Fine $500,000 if an individual, $2 million if other than individual
Hashish	10 kg or less		
Hashish Oil	1 kg or less		

APPENDIX 2

STATE COCAINE SENTENCING POLICY

States	Summary of Statutory Differences
Alabama	The penalties for crack and powder cocaine are the same but the state uses a 10-to-1 drug quantity ratio to determine eligibility for the drug abuse diversion program. The penalties range from a mandatory minimum three years imprisonment for between 28 and 500 grams to a mandatory 15-year term for one to 10 kilograms. To be eligible for the program, the quantity of powder cocaine cannot exceed five grams. The maximum quantity of crack cocaine is 500 milligrams (one-half gram).
Arizona	Uses a drug quantity ratio of 12-to-1 to distinguish powder and crack cocaine offenses. Nine grams of powder cocaine or 750 milligrams of crack is the threshold for trafficking, which carries a presumptive sentence of five years imprisonment.
California	Sentences for possession or possession with intent to sell are treated differently based on the form of cocaine involved. Crack cocaine offenders are subject to a three, four, or five-year term while powder cocaine offender are subject to two, three, or four-year terms. Absent mitigating or aggravating factors, offenders receive the middle sentence. Although the ranges fluctuate, a crack cocaine offender in effect serves 1. 25 to 1. 5 times longer than a powder cocaine offender.

Connecticut	Uses a 56. 7-to-1 drug quantity ratio to distinguish trafficking offenses involving crack and powder cocaine. The penalty for selling one ounce or more of powder cocaine or . 5 grams of crack is five years to life imprisonment.
Iowa	Uses a 100-to-1 drug quantity ratio to distinguish offenses involving crack and powder cocaine. Instead of triggering mandatory minimum penalties, the ratio is reflected in the threshold for the maximum statutory penalty. Possession of more than five kilograms of cocaine or more than 50 grams of crack is punishable by a maximum penalty of 50 years imprisonment. Possession of more than 500 grams of powder or more than five grams of crack carries a maximum penalty of 25 years imprisonment.
Maine	Uses a 3. 5-to-1 drug quantity ratio to distinguish trafficking offenses involving crack and powder cocaine. Possession of 14 grams or more of powder cocaine or four grams or more of crack establishes a presumption of trafficking. Aggravated trafficking (i. e. , 112 grams of powder or 32 grams of crack) carries a mandatory minimum sentence of four years imprisonment.
Maryland	Uses a 9-to-1 drug quantity ratio to distinguish trafficking offenses involving crack and powder cocaine. Trafficking 448 grams or more of powder or 50 grams of crack carries a five-year mandatory minimum.

200

Missouri	Uses a 75-to-1 drug quantity ratio to differentiate between offenses involving crack and powder cocaine. Trafficking between 150 and 450 grams of powder cocaine or between two and six grams of crack is a Class A felony, punishable by 10 to 30 years imprisonment. Offenders who sell more than these maximum amounts are ineligible for probation or parole.
New Hampshire	Uses a 28-to-1 drug quantity ratio to distinguish trafficking offenses involving crack and powder cocaine. Trafficking in five or more ounces of powder cocaine or five or more grams of crack is punishable by up to 30 years imprisonment.
Oklahoma	Uses a 6-to-1 drug quantity ratio to differentiate between offenses involving crack and powder cocaine. Mandatory 10-year prison term for offenses involving 28 or more grams of powder cocaine or five or more grams of crack. Mandatory 20-year prison term for offenses involving 300 or more grams of powder cocaine or 50 or more grams of crack.
South Carolina	A first time offender possessing 10 grains (.648 grams) or less of powder cocaine is subject to a maximum two-year prison term while the same offender with less than one gram of crack is subject to a maximum five-year term. Distribution crimes do not differ between the two forms of cocaine.
Virginia	No distinction between offenses involving the two forms of cocaine. However, the "drug kingpin" statute does differentiate, using a 2-to-1 drug quantity ratio. Under this statute, an offender who traffics five kilograms or more of powder cocaine or 2.5 kilograms or more of crack is subject to a 20-year mandatory minimum sentence.

INDEX

INDEX

INDEX

INDEX

INDEX

INDEX

INDEX

INDEX

INDEX

INDEX

ALPHABETICAL INDEX OF 100 'MOST ASKED' QUESTIONS...

INDEX

ALPHABETICAL INDEX OF 100 'MOST ASKED' QUESTIONS...

INDEX

ALPHABETICAL INDEX OF 100 'MOST ASKED' QUESTIONS...

INDEX

ALPHABETICAL INDEX OF 100 'MOST ASKED' QUESTIONS...

NOTES:

The information and materials provided in this book are based on:

California Penal Code, Title 1, Title 7, Title 8, Title 13
Federal Criminal Code, Title 18
Federal Pattern Jury Instructions for the 11th Circuit
Florida criminal statutes and Standard Jury Instructions
Illinois 720 ILCS 5, Criminal Code of 1961 rev.
Model Laws from the American Law Institute
New York Penal Code
Texas Penal Code, Title 2, Title 5, Title 7, et seq.
U.S. Supreme Court case law

Laws are different in each of the 50 states and the U.S. Federal courts.
An attorney licensed in the jurisdiction in which your matter is litigated is the only person who can provide you with legal advice and a legal opinion. Consult an attorney in your state for assistance.
This book is not a substitute for legal advice.